FRONTLINE
COVERAGE OF CURRENT EVENTS™

GUANTÁNAMO BAY AND MILITARY TRIBUNALS

THE DETENTION AND TRIAL OF SUSPECTED TERRORISTS

Bill Scheppler

The Rosen Publishing Group, Inc., New York

Published in 2005 by The Rosen Publishing Group, Inc.
29 East 21st Street, New York, NY 10010

Copyright © 2005 by The Rosen Publishing Group, Inc.

First Edition

Library of Congress Cataloging-in-Publication Data

Scheppler, Bill.
Guantánamo Bay and military tribunals: the detention and trial of suspected terrorists/ Bill Scheppler.
    p. cm.—(Frontline coverage of current events)
Includes bibliographical references and index.
ISBN 1-4042-0278-1 (library binding)
1. Terrorism investigation—United States. 2. Terrorists—Government policy— United States. 3. Military courts—United States. 4. Detention of persons—United States. 5. Aliens—Government policy—United States. 6. September 11 Terrorist Attacks, 2001.
I. Title. II. Series.
HV8079.T47S34 2005
973.931—dc22

2004008424

Manufactured in the United States of America

On the cover: Foreground: Military police escort a detainee in Camp Delta at Guantánamo Bay Detention Center in February 2002. Background: The razor-wire fence and a watchtower at Camp Delta.

Contents

Introduction: A Detention Center for
the U.S. War on Terrorism   4

1   U.S. Military Detention Center
at Guantánamo Bay   6

2   Prisoners of War
or Enemy Combatants   13

3   Life in a Detention Center   20

4   Understanding Military Tribunals   26

5   What Lies Ahead for
Guantánamo Bay Detainees   33

Glossary   40

For More Information   43

For Further Reading   44

Bibliography   45

Index   47

Introduction

A Detention Center for the U.S. War on Terrorism

An extended stay on a Caribbean island represents paradise to millions of vacationers every year, but to just less than 600 men detained at Guantánamo Bay, Cuba—the largest island in the region—represents prison, plain and simple. The men are labeled "enemy combatants." They were captured and detained by U.S. and coalition forces in America's war on terrorism. The majority of them spend their days sitting in prison cells. The state of affairs at the Guantánamo Bay Detention Center is a study in contrasts.

International debates are raging over the United States' decision to detain enemy combatants at Guantánamo Bay, and the questions are endless. Why is the U.S. government holding detainees outside the control of its own federal courts? Why did President George W. Bush make the decision to refuse all detainees prisoner-of-war status in glaring violation of the Geneva Conventions? Why did the president declare U.S. citizens enemy combatants and sentence them indefinitely, exercising authority

The entrance to the permanent detention center called Camp Delta at Guantánamo Bay, Cuba, is heavily barricaded by a razor-wire and chain-link fence. The detention center holds detainees from the U.S. war on terrorism, most of whom were captured in Afghanistan in 2002.

not granted by the U.S. Constitution? This book provides a good understanding of how the United States arrived at the current situation and prepares readers for the history-making events that are right around the corner.

chapter 1
U.S. Military Detention Center at Guantánamo Bay

Inside a holding area at U.S. Naval Base Guantánamo Bay's Camp X-Ray, naval military police watch over the first detainees from Afghanistan in January 2002. The majority of the detainees are accused by the United States of being either Taliban soldiers or Al Qaeda terrorist operatives.

The first twenty prisoners of America's war on terrorism to be held behind the razor-wire fences of the U.S. military detention center at Guantánamo Bay arrived from Kandahar, Afghanistan, on January 11, 2002. Since then, the eyes of the world have been focused on this southeastern corner of Cuba. For more than a century, this strategically positioned Caribbean port has been home to one of the United States' most renowned naval stations. With its ideal location, existing facilities, and expert personnel, the U.S. Naval Base Guantánamo Bay (GTMO, or Gitmo) is uniquely equipped to assume the responsibility of its current mission.

In the winter of 1927, 210 ships from the Atlantic and Pacific fleets of the U.S. Navy held joint maneuvers in Guantánamo Bay. American ships still use the U.S. naval base, called Gitmo, as a refueling station, and as a place to restock their supplies of fresh water and provisions.

Establishing a Naval Base

Guantánamo Bay has a colorful history that stretches back to 1494. At that time, during his second voyage from Spain to the New World, Christopher Columbus sailed into and documented the port that he called "Puerto Grande." The following centuries saw Guantánamo Bay acting as a haven and a hideout for seafaring vessels. British and Spanish forces clashed for control over the harbor several times in the early eighteenth century. When the British pulled out in 1741, Spain gained a foothold that it would retain for the next 157 years.

Spanish rule in Cuba ended in 1898. This was brought on by an uprising of Cuban rebels fighting to overthrow their Spanish occupiers. The United States had a strong interest in this island just 200 miles (322 kilometers) off the southern tip of Florida. The United States took

The U.S. Naval Base Guantánamo Bay is located on the southeastern end of Cuba in Guantánamo Province. Cuba, an island in the Greater Antilles, West Indies, lies about 200 miles (322 km) off the southern coast of Florida. The United States negotiated a permanent lease for Guantánamo Bay with the Republic of Cuba in 1903.

the side of the rebels and in 1898 declared war on Spain (known today as the Spanish-American War). The U.S. Navy successfully blockaded Havana harbor to the north, then pursued the Spanish navy south and into Santiago Bay, where it secured the enemy fleet. Once in control, U.S. forces established a naval base at Guantánamo Bay. Spain surrendered later that year. In 1903, using as leverage the fact that it already controlled the territory, the United States negotiated a permanent lease for GTMO with Cuba, which had become an independent republic in 1902.

Those familiar with the U.S. Naval Base Guantánamo Bay refer to it by its abbreviation, "Gitmo." The United States and Cuba strengthened their agreement over Gitmo with the Treaty of 1934. Every year, the United States pays the Cuban government to lease the land at Guantánamo Bay, but Cuba retains sovereignty, or governmental authority. (The payment indicated in the original agreement was $2,000 in gold coins, but today the payment is closer to the amount of $4,000.) This agreement cannot be broken unless both parties agree to break it. Gitmo's primary mission is to function as a refueling and maintenance port for U.S. ships. It also plays an important role in policing illegal drug trafficking into the United

In 1992, Haitian refugees sought shelter in a camp in Guantánamo Bay after a bloody military coup ousted Haiti's president, Jean-Bertrand Aristide, in 1991. The Haitians were waiting for processing as refugees by U.S. authorities. The U.S. Navy's Joint Task Force 160 provided care for more than 50,000 refugees.

States. Since the early 1990s, Gitmo has been a temporary refugee camp for Cuban and Haitian migrants, providing food, shelter, and care for tens of thousands of people.

Destination for Detainees

Gitmo is not the only detention center used by the United States to house prisoners of its war on terrorism. During the war on terror so far,

U.S. and coalition forces have held more than 10,000 detainees at centers in Afghanistan, Iraq, and elsewhere. However, the captives transferred to Gitmo are considered the most dangerous, with the most valuable information on terrorist operations. In December 2001, U.S. Secretary of Defense Donald H. Rumsfeld referred to Gitmo as the "least worst place we could have selected," but there are several reasons to think Gitmo may have been the best option.

Gitmo's location is a benefit—a three-hour flight from Florida makes travel convenient for U.S. authorities, inspectors, and legal teams who routinely make the trek to and from the base. Gitmo's security is the best. U.S.-Cuban relations collapsed with Communist dictator Fidel Castro's rise to power in the Cuban Revolution of 1959. The new enemies spent most of the Cold War building defenses to protect against attack—most notably during the Bay of Pigs invasion in 1961 and the Cuban missile crisis in 1962. Today, with 17 miles (27.4 km) of razor-wire fence on the U.S. side, an equal amount on the Cuban side, and strategically placed cactus fields and landmines in between, it is as difficult to gain access into Gitmo as it is to escape from it.

Existing facilities and personnel also helped to swing the detention decision in favor of Gitmo. There are more similarities than differences between a refugee camp and a detention center. At the height of Operation Sea Signal (from 1994 to 1996), Gitmo had assembled the resources to support more than 50,000 refugees who came from Caribbean nations such as Haiti and Cuba seeking political protection in the United States. Upon the arrival of the first detainees from the war on terrorism in January 2002, Gitmo housed only forty-eight refugees, so it was a simple task to convert a section of the base known as Camp X-Ray into a temporary detention center. The U.S. Navy personnel and marines responsible for the care of refugees (known as Joint Task Force 160) assumed their new mission: providing the same services for detainees.

Permanent Detention Center

The arrival of detainees brought not only the focus of the eyes of the

INSIDE THE CENTER: IBRAHIM AHMED MAHMOUD AL-QOSI

On February 24, 2004, the U.S. government charged Gitmo detainee Ibrahim Ahmed Mahmoud al-Qosi with conspiracy to commit war crimes. According to U.S. intelligence, al-Qosi is originally from Sudan and joined Al Qaeda in 1989. A trained accountant, al-Qosi held various jobs for Al Qaeda from courier to financial officer to personal bodyguard for Osama bin Laden, the head of the terrorist organization. While running Al Qaeda's finances, al-Qosi managed the money that Al Qaeda received from several Muslim charities and signed checks on behalf of bin Laden. Al-Qosi completed military exercises at an Al Qaeda training camp and is believed to have worn an explosive belt when protecting the Al Qaeda leader.

world on Gitmo but also the scrutiny of human rights organizations. The temporary detention center at Camp X-Ray drew criticism from the first day. Its outdoor cells, which measured 6 feet by 8 feet (1.8 meters by 2.4 meters) and had chain-link walls and wooden roofs, were called scandalous cages, offering little protection from the elements. The Pentagon halted the arrival of new captives in mid-January 2002 and allowed the International Committee of the Red Cross, U.S. senators, and British officials to inspect the facility and provide recommendations for improvement. It should be noted that during this time, the U.S. military personnel providing security at Camp X-Ray were occupying makeshift quarters as well—living in tents with no indoor plumbing or access to hot water.

Construction on a permanent detention center began in late

A detention cell at Camp Delta, such as the one pictured here, includes a bed, a flush toilet, and a sink with running water that is fit for drinking. Each cell measures 7 by 8 feet (2.1 by 2.4 m). *Inset*: On arrival at Camp Delta, each detainee receives an orange jumpsuit, towels, flip-flops, soap, shampoo, sheets, a blanket, and supplemental food items.

is an improvement over Camp X-Ray. By the end of April, all detainees had been moved to the new 7-by-8-foot (2.1-by-2.4-m) cells, which include accommodations such as flush toilets, sinks with running water, and beds with mattresses, sheets, and blankets. Built off the ground with a steel frame construction, sealed roofs, and metal-mesh unit separators, the detention blocks at Camp Delta offer far greater shelter from wind, rain, and sun than the temporary units at Camp X-Ray. Camp X-Ray closed for good on April 29, 2002.

February, one month after the Red Cross's inspection. The result is Camp Delta. Although it retains the function of a prison, the new facility

chapter 2

Prisoners of War or Enemy Combatants

In December 2001, two anti-Taliban fighters captured an Arab member of Al Qaeda in the mountainous region of Tora Bora in Afghanistan. Osama bin Laden, who is blamed for the September 11, 2001, terrorist attacks on the United States, and his Al Qaeda fighters were thought to have fled to the caves of Tora Bora during the U.S. and British bombing campaign in Afghanistan.

"Prisoner of war" and "enemy combatant" are two legal status options for detainees captured during international armed conflict. The decision over which status applies to the detainees at Gitmo is one of the most complex rulings the United States Supreme Court has had to make regarding the war on terrorism. Warfare has rules, which are recorded in a series of international treaties known as the Geneva Conventions. However, the war on terrorism is like nothing the world has known. As a result, some previously accepted rules of combat may no longer apply. Until the Geneva Conventions, which were established between 1864 and 1949, evolve to catch up with the current international landscape, these decisions will be hotly debated.

On August 12, 1949, members of the international conference that was held in Geneva, Switzerland, signed the four Geneva Conventions. These international treaties bound all countries who accepted them to the rules of humanitarian law. The four Geneva Conventions included international rules about the treatment of soldiers and sailors who become wounded or sick during war, the rights of prisoners of war, and the protection of civilians during war.

The Geneva Conventions

The United States and Afghanistan adopted the third Geneva Convention on August 12, 1949. The third Geneva Convention directly addresses the legal status of prisoners of war. In it, the document states that people who fall into the power of the enemy and obey one or more of the following standards must be considered prisoners of war: observance of a clear commander, wearing of a fixed distinctive sign or insignia recognizable at a distance, carrying of arms openly, and conducting operations in accordance of the laws and customs of war. If a person falls into the power of the enemy and cannot be classified as a prisoner of war, then a military court also known as a tribunal must determine his or her status.

Prisoners of war are considered "lawful combatants" and are granted certain basic rights under the Geneva Conventions. "Unlawful combatants," or what the United States refers to as enemy combatants, are not. The U.S. Supreme Court applied the term during a 1942 decision (*Ex Parte Quirin*) that states: "An enemy combatant who without uniform comes secretly through the lines for the purpose of waging war by destruction of life or property are familiar examples of belligerents [criminals] who are generally deemed not to be entitled to the status of prisoners of war, but to be offenders against the law of war subject to trial and punishment by military tribunals."

The majority of detainees at Guantánamo Bay are accused of being either Taliban soldiers or Al Qaeda terrorist operatives. Moreover, they have all been labeled enemy combatants by President George W. Bush, which means that they are not protected by the third Geneva Convention. All of them could face punishment by military tribunals. There are clear differences between the Taliban and Al Qaeda—differences that hold significance in their members' legal status as wartime detainees.

Exploring the Distinction

The first step in understanding President Bush's decision to categorize detainees at Gitmo as enemy combatants is to identify America's enemies in its war on terrorism. America's primary enemy is Al Qaeda, which is Arabic for "the base" or "the foundation," the religious, independent military organization founded by Osama bin Laden in 1988 to assist in driving Soviet occupiers out of Afghanistan.

INSIDE THE CENTER: JOINT TASK FORCE COMMANDER GEOFFREY MILLER

Major General Geoffrey Miller assumed command of the Joint Task Force (JTF) in November 2002. Responsible for all Gitmo detention and interrogation operations, he played a key role in defining lawful rules for interrogation. Miller remained in command until March 2004, when he was transferred to Iraq to take over detention operations at Abu Ghraib military prison near Baghdad. Prior to Miller's transfer, Abu Ghraib was the site of shocking prisoner abuses at the hands of U.S. military personnel. The *New York Times* reported on May 13, 2004, that after a visit to Abu Ghraib in August 2003, Miller recommended procedures for getting intelligence information from the prisoners there, some of which were based on aggressive interrogation techniques that he had instituted at Gitmo. At present it is not known whether Miller's recommended changes directly contributed to the abuses that occurred at the prison in December 2003. Some of these abuses included the use of hoods on prisoners, sleep deprivation, and physical and sexual abuse. Miller insisted that the recommendations he gave in 2003 were in line with the Geneva Conventions. In his role as chief of interrogations and detentions in Iraq, Miller established a permanent International Red Cross presence at Abu Ghraib, revised the U.S. Army's interrogation manual, and ensured that all prisoners were held in accordance with the Geneva Conventions. Brigadier General Jay W. Hood replaced Miller as JTF Commander at Gitmo on March 24, 2004.

Ironically, the United States was a financial supporter of Al Qaeda at the time because it shared an interest in the Soviet Union's defeat. Al Qaeda's current goal is to spread the Wahhabi theology across the Muslim world. (Wahhabism is a fundamentalist movement of Islam and was founded in Saudi Arabia. Wahhabis consider their religion the true form of Islam.) To this end, in 1998, bin Laden issued a statement calling on all Muslims to "kill U.S. citizens, either civilian or military, and their allies everywhere."

Although Al Qaeda has been in existence for more than fifteen years, is well funded, and boasts thousands of trained fighters, it would be difficult to argue that its members who are held captive at Gitmo deserve prisoner-of-war status. According to the Geneva Conventions, a prisoner of war must represent a territory. In contrast, Al Qaeda represents a religion and asserts that it has

members around the world including in the United States. A prisoner of war must wear a uniform or at least a distinctive sign recognizable from a distance; Al Qaeda members try to blend in with civilians when executing a terrorist attack. Prisoners of war must respect the laws and customs of war; Al Qaeda operatives do not.

If the United States held tribunals to determine whether Al Qaeda detainees are labeled prisoners of war or enemy combatants, the U.S. government would likely receive the enemy combatant classification it seeks. As an added benefit, the United States would win the support of the international community by coming into accordance with the Geneva Conventions. Determining the status of members of the Taliban is a slightly different matter.

America's secondary enemy is the Taliban, which is an Islamic fundamentalist militia that came to

GARMABAK GHAR TERRORIST TRAINING CAMP, AFGHANISTAN
PRE STRIKE

GARMABAK GHAR TERRORIST TRAINING CAMP, AFGHANISTAN
POST STRIKE

Top: This satellite image shows a terrorist training camp in Garmabak Ghar, near the Taliban city of Kandahar, Afghanistan, before U.S. and British air strikes on October 9, 2001. After the September 11, 2001, terrorist attacks on the United States, coalition forces joined in a military mission called Operation Enduring Freedom, which included destroying Taliban and Al Qaeda terrorist training camps. *Bottom*: This satellite image shows the same training camp after coalition air missiles struck it on October 9, 2001.

power during Afghanistan's civil war, set up an Islamic government that enforced a severe Muslim code of behavior, and ruled Afghanistan from 1996 to 2001. The Taliban was closely associated with Al Qaeda, which continued to operate training camps in the country after the Soviet forces withdrew in 1989. Following Al Qaeda's terrorist attacks on the World Trade Center in New York

City and the Pentagon outside Washington, D.C., on September 11, 2001, the U.S. military bombed the mountainous regions of Afghanistan, where it believed Osama bin Laden to be hiding. Soon after, the United States sent in ground forces to destroy Al Qaeda training camps, freeze its assets, and seize evidence. Taliban members fought alongside Al Qaeda operatives against the superior forces of the U.S. military and its allies. Although Taliban soldiers did not wear uniforms, an argument could be made that at least some Taliban detainees at Gitmo deserve prisoner-of-war status because several countries, including Pakistan and Saudi Arabia, recognized the Taliban as Afghanistan's ruling government. However, until the United States holds tribunals to determine classification of Taliban detainees, this argument will remain unheard.

According to a letter President Bush wrote to Congress on September 20, 2002, he and his administration are committed to treating all Taliban and Al Qaeda detainees in Guantánamo Bay "humanely and, to the extent appropriate and consistent with military necessity, in a manner consistent with the principles of the Geneva Conventions of 1949." These conventions will be reviewed and may be amended as soon as world leaders make some sense out of an era of war with indistinct battlefields and ill-defined sides.

chapter 3
Life in a Detention Center

U.S. troops capture a suspected Al Qaeda or Taliban fighter in southeastern Afghanistan during Operation Alamo Sweep in November 2002. The screening team that questions captives at a center near the battlefield determines the status of the detainee, including whether he should be released or transferred to Gitmo, depending on the information obtained during that detainee's interviews.

Capturing and detaining members of an opponent's fighting force has always been a part of war. Every detainee represents one less threat on the battlefield and one more opportunity to gain invaluable enemy intelligence. When facing a terrorist network as secretive and widespread as Al Qaeda, each detainee—and the information he possesses—becomes even more important. As of October 2004, just fewer than 600 captives remain in custody at Gitmo, where military specialists conduct interviews with them to find out what they know about Al Qaeda, its leaders, and future terrorist activities. Because women are restricted from participating in Al Qaeda and the Taliban, all Gitmo detainees are men. Although most were apprehended in Afghanistan and Pakistan, they represent more than forty countries.

The Path to Guantánamo Bay

After the September 11, 2001, terrorist attacks on U.S. soil, the American-led forces swept across Afghanistan. The first wave of the invasion resulted in the capture of rank-and-file foot soldiers as well as senior Al Qaeda operatives, Taliban leaders, and many innocent civilians caught on the battlefield. To ensure that noncombatants are released and only the highest-ranking captives are sent to Gitmo, the United States initiated an elaborate detainee-screening process, which works as follows:

Soldiers in the field interview each detainee. After a report on his capture is drafted, the captive is transported to a central holding area. There, a screening team made up of U.S. intelligence officials, military lawyers, and federal law enforcement officials reviews the detainee's status and may conduct further interviews. This team weighs the threat posed by the detainee, speculates as to the amount of intelligence he may hold, and makes a recommendation for release or transfer to Gitmo. If the recommendation is for transfer to Gitmo, then a combatant commander further assesses the detainee and presents his decision to a Department of Defense panel. It is this panel that makes the final decision on whether or not to relocate the individual to Gitmo. Less than 10 percent of detainees are sent to Guantánamo Bay. The rest are returned to their country of citizenship for prosecution or simply released if they do not pose a threat.

Transfer to Guantánamo Bay for those detainees considered the greatest threat to U.S. and coalition forces is a difficult experience. Most flights to the detention center take off under cover of night. The trip from the U.S.-controlled airfield at

On January 11, 2002, the first twenty detainees from Afghanistan arrived at the U.S. Naval Base Guantánamo Bay, in Cuba. U.S. forces captured the suspected Al Qaeda terrorists during combat in Afghanistan. While in detention at Gitmo, the prisoners were interrogated about terrorist activities and questioned about their alleged connection to Osama bin Laden.

Kandahar in Afghanistan to the Guantánamo Bay detention camp is about 8,000 miles (12,875 km). Reports indicate that manacles bind the detainees' hands and feet for the entire twenty-hour trip—they may not leave their seats, so provisions are made when they must use a toilet. Prior to boarding the aircraft, detainees are shaved head-to-toe for hygiene purposes. They wear orange jumpsuits to increase visibility and tape-covered goggles to reduce vision. They might also wear surgical masks to prevent the spread of airborne germs. Detainees sit back-to-back on the flight and are under the constant surveillance of military guards until their arrival at Gitmo.

Accommodations for Detainees

Camp Delta features multiple security levels, improved meals and health care, and an increased cultural understanding between guards and detainees. The detention center at Gitmo is a highly secure military prison constructed to hold terrorists that the U.S. government considers to be some of the most dangerous men in the world. Nevertheless, it should be noted that efforts have been made to address the basic needs of all detainees and to reward cooperation with additional comforts and privileges.

Camp Delta was constructed in five phases that resulted in five sub-camps. Camp One is a high-security area, Camp Two and Camp Three are maximum security sectors, Camp Four is a medium-security camp, where bunkhouses replace cell blocks, and Camp Five is a permanent facility constructed of concrete and steel. The conditions in Camp One, Camp Two, and Camp Three are similar. Lights remain on day and night, guards are on constant patrol, and detainees are allowed out of their cells for thirty minutes of exercise just three times a week. Exercise takes place in a fenced pen that measures 25 feet by 30 feet (7.6 m by 9.1 m). After exercise, detainees are allowed a five-minute supervised shower. Maximum-security detainees exercise alone, whereas high-security detainees may exercise in pairs.

Detainees who obey the rules of the camp and cooperate with U.S. interrogators receive rewards such as access to board games and books and mail service provided by the Red Cross (incoming and outgoing letters are censored by Gitmo authorities). The best perk is a transfer to Camp Four. Detainees live in groups at Camp Four. The men are free to move indoors and

ADDRESSING THE NEEDS OF MUSLIM DETAINEES

A U.S. Navy chaplain (*left*), who is Muslim, conducts morning prayers at Gitmo in January 2002.

Muslims obey strict tenets over prayer and diet. Because all Gitmo detainees follow the Muslim faith, the United States made special accommodations for their spiritual needs. It is customary for Muslims to pray five times daily, while kneeling on a prayer mat and facing the holy city of Mecca in Saudi Arabia. To that end, each detainee possesses in his cell the Koran, a prayer mat, and a prayer cap. An arrow painted on the cell floor points in the direction of Mecca, and announcements over the camp's broadcast system indicate when it is time to begin a prayer session. In addition, all meat prepared for the detainees is Halal, which means the animals were slaughtered in accordance with Muslim tradition.

outdoors as they please. Besides daily exercise and shower privileges, they receive supplemental food items with their meals. Lightweight white clothing and canvas shoes replace the polyester orange uniforms and flip-flops worn by detainees in the other camps, which make the Caribbean heat more bearable. The most worthwhile

A detainee is being escorted to a medium security camp at Gitmo. Detainees who live at minimum and medium facilities, such as at Camp Four, a medium security camp, wear white clothing instead of the orange jumpsuits worn at a maximum security camp. Detainees in Camp Four live in a communal environment and are allowed to exercise in groups and have more contact with fellow detainees than in other camps.

reward is the regular contact with their fellow detainees.

Camp Five, which opened in May 2004 following nine months of construction, is the first detention facility at Gitmo designed to hold prisoners for long periods of time. This multiwinged complex encompasses approximately 24,000 square feet (2,230 sq m), housing a modern interrogation facility and cells for 100 detainees.

chapter 4
Understanding Military Tribunals

U.S. Marine Corps Major Michael Mori speaks to reporters at a news conference in Arlington, Virginia, in 2004. Mori is the military lawyer for David Hicks, an Australian who U.S. authorities have formally charged with conspiracy to commit war crimes, attempted murder, and aiding the enemy. Hicks may be tried as an enemy combatant in the first U.S. military tribunal since World War II.

President George W. Bush declared in his Military Order of November 13, 2001, that enemy combatants detained by the United States who are charged with war crimes will be tried by military tribunals. A military tribunal is a special judicial process that is used in unique cases when other judicial options are not valid. These other options include the U.S. criminal court system or a military court-martial. By holding detainees outside U.S. jurisdiction and labeling them enemy combatants rather than prisoners of war, American authorities removed those other options, leaving tribunals as the only judicial choice. Traditional military tribunals are similar to courts-martial, but critics note several differences that reduce a defendant's chance of an impartial trial. Tribunals do not include an appeals process. In response to such criticism, the Pentagon revised the tribunal procedures for Gitmo detainees to address international fairness concerns.

Who Will Face Tribunals?

Only detainees meeting the following criteria outlined in President Bush's military order are eligible to face tribunals for war crimes: The individual must not be a U.S. citizen; there must be reason to believe the individual is or was a member of Al Qaeda; he must have engaged in, assisted with, or conspired to commit acts of international terrorism against the United States; or he knowingly harbored one or more of these individuals. In addition, it must be in the interest of the United States that the individual be subject to stand trial. Ideally, if an enemy combatant is subject to the military order, these questions were answered during his screening interviews prior to transfer to Guantánamo Bay, so that when he lands at the detention center, the

This courtroom at Guantánamo Bay will be used for the U.S. military tribunals for war crimes. A military commission, consisting of three to seven military officers, will vote on findings during the trial and recommend a sentence if a guilty verdict is reached.

focus at Gitmo turns to compiling evidence for the trial.

The lack of direct evidence connecting individual war crimes to Gitmo detainees may be because many of these combatants are allegedly senior operatives, which means they would have been involved in planning crimes but not necessarily in carrying out the actions. Interrogation is used for

Military police (MP) escort a Gitmo detainee to an interrogation room in February 2002. At that time, there were 158 detainees being held at Gitmo. In October 2004, there were 550 detainees being held as enemy combatants.

gathering bits of information from detainees and piecing them together to gain an overall understanding of Al Qaeda and to build individual cases. These intense interviews, which may last up to sixteen hours in a single day, are conducted by Joint Task Force 170 (the U.S. military personnel at Gitmo responsible for interrogation) and the Criminal Investigative Task Force. The

Criminal Investigative Task Force is made up of military intelligence specialists, the FBI, and law enforcement agencies. The tribunal's chief prosecutor receives the combined data and presents it to the appointing authority who decides whether the evidence is adequate to charge the detainee with a crime.

Intelligence teams take as much time gathering and evaluating evidence as is necessary to ensure that they make sound decisions. However, representatives of human rights groups, such as Amnesty International and Fair Trials Abroad, and countries such as Great Britain that have citizens in detention at Gitmo are critical of the lengthy interrogation process. This process dragged on for two years without a single formal charge being made or a tribunal being held. In a mid-February 2004 response, Defense Secretary Rumsfeld assured critics that the process is working, valuable intelligence continues to flow, and "U.S. officials have no desire to hold enemy combatants longer than necessary." Finally, on February 24, 2004, the Pentagon charged two men with conspiracy to commit war crimes. Ali Hamza Ahmed Sulayman al-Bahlul of Yemen and Ibrahim Ahmed Mahmoud al-Qosi of Sudan are the first detainees to face military tribunals in America's war on terrorism.

Detainees selected to face tribunals are immediately transferred from Camp Delta to nearby Camp Echo, where they are held in solitary confinement, under twenty-four-hour surveillance. Individual cells feature adjoining meeting rooms where prisoners may meet with lawyers to prepare for the tribunal proceedings. Although solitary conditions are particularly harsh for prisoners, they are necessary to keep precommission detainees separate from the general prison population, which may attempt to persuade them against testifying, and they allow for semi-private legal counsel.

Overview of the "Commissions" Process

The United States has not held military tribunals since *Ex Parte Quirin*, a 1942 U.S. Supreme Court case involving German saboteurs caught entering the United States with bomb-detonating materials

This April 2004 photograph shows an interrogation room at Camp Delta. The ring that is fastened to the floor holds a detainee's shackles for restraining him.

during World War II. Although international law has evolved greatly over the past sixty years, *Ex Parte Quirin* remains relevant as a precedent for conducting tribunals today. The case had some negative aspects as well: the trial was held in secrecy and resulted in the execution of six defendants five days after their conviction. Two informants, who traded testimony for pardon, each received thirty-year prison sentences. To distance today's tribunals from *Ex Parte Quirin*, the Bush administration in its initial military commission regulations

document, issued on March 21, 2001, dropped the term "military tribunals" in favor of "military commissions," which it considers less controversial. We, too, will refer to tribunals as commissions for the remainder of this book.

The appointing authority approves and files charges against a detainee. Then the appointing authority must assemble the military commission, ensure that the prosecution and defense have appropriate resources to carry out their duties and set a trial date. A military commission consists of three to seven military officers, at least one of whom is an active judge advocate (military attorney) who serves as the presiding officer. The commission votes on findings during the trial and recommends a sentence if a guilty verdict is reached. After a trial, the appointing authority reviews all court records and either returns the case to the commission for further proceedings or approves the records and forwards the case to a review panel.

The U.S. secretary of defense appoints three civilians to serve a two-year term on the review panel. At least one member must have prior experience as a judge, and all three receive military officer rank and security clearance for the duration of the term. This panel hears any additional matters submitted by the defense or prosecution and reviews the case for material errors of law. The panel may return the case to the commission for further proceedings or forward it to the defense secretary. On review, the defense secretary requests additional proceedings or submits the case to the U.S. president for a final verdict. The president may approve or reject the findings; change a finding of guilty to a lesser offense; or mitigate, defer, commute, or suspend the sentence. The president may not, however, change a "not guilty" verdict to "guilty." The president also has the option of returning the case to the military commission for further proceedings or removing himself from the process and assigning final approval to the U.S. secretary of state.

Military Commission Instructions

The U.S. Department of Defense (DOD) published a series of eight military commission instruction documents in April 2003 and one review document in December 2003. These documents explain in detail the procedures for the military commissions in trying enemy combatants during America's war on terrorism. The DOD attempted to develop a process that was as fair and open as possible without sacrificing the security requirements of a nation engaged in active war. However, legal experts will argue over the balance between civil rights and national security for as long as the trials take place. As this book is in progress on the eve of the initial military commissions at Guantánamo Bay, the outcome remains to be seen; therefore, the debate remains relevant.

The instruction documents include procedural safeguards that are similar to U.S. criminal court cases and courts-martial but are also unique because of the sensitivity of the evidence and the potential threat to the people involved. Defendants are presumed innocent until proven guilty beyond a reasonable doubt. Guilt must be determined by two-thirds of the military commissions, rather than unanimously as in U.S. criminal courts. A defendant is provided with a military defense counsel at no cost to assist him in preparing his defense. However, if he chooses, he may hire a civilian defense counsel so long as that counsel fulfills the requirements of the commissions. These requirements include eligibility for at least a military secret-level security clearance. Commissions may be closed to the public at times to protect classified information, witnesses, and methods used in gathering intelligence. The death penalty is recognized as a sentencing option. In addition, standards for admitting evidence are lower than in U.S. criminal courts, taking into account the unique battlefield environment where warfare and search warrants rarely mix.

chapter 5

What Lies Ahead for Guantánamo Bay Detainees

A guard at Gitmo watches detainees sitting in a holding area in January 2002.

All Gitmo detainees are recognized as enemy combatants in America's war on terrorism, but not all detainees will be charged with war crimes and face military commissions. International laws of armed conflict, which include rules for detaining enemy combatants, permit active war parties to hold enemies without charges for the duration of the conflict. The United States will do so as long as those detainees pose a significant threat to its military forces, citizens, and coalition partners. However, the United States is not interested in holding any detainee longer than necessary. To that end, on February 13, 2004, Defense Secretary Rumsfeld announced the creation of annual detainee reviews during which all available information on a detainee will be reviewed to determine his future status.

Annual Detainee Review

Detainees are under constant evaluation by a team of interrogators, analysts, behavioral scientists, and regional experts. These specialists assess each enemy combatant's intelligence value, law enforcement interest, and level of threat. They combine their findings to build cases against individual detainees. Once complete, the case is forwarded to Southern Command (the U.S. military's unified command with jurisdiction over Guantánamo Bay) for review and detainee status recommendation. The commander of Southern Command then presents the recommendation to a Washington, D.C., committee. This committee consists of intelligence, law enforcement, and defense representatives. The committee members review the case together to form a unified assessment and present their decision to the defense secretary. Based on this

information, the defense secretary decides whether the detainee is released, transferred to the custody of his home country, or further detained at Guantánamo Bay.

Usually enemy combatants who remain in detention at Gitmo either hold substantial intelligence value or pose a significant threat. However, over time—through further interrogation or other means—the detainee's status may change. The annual review process ensures that each detainee's status is reassessed at least once each year. A review board, composed of three military officers who report to a designated civilian official, conducts annual reviews. A detainee may appear before the board to make a statement on his behalf, and his home government has the opportunity to submit information as well. The board considers these presentations, along with information from interagency sources, and recommends whether the detainee be

A detainee at Gitmo reads while listening to an official read the Defense Department's Combatant Status Review Tribunal Notice of July 7, 2004. Under international pressure and after the U.S. Supreme Court's ruling in June 2004 that Guantánamo Bay detainees should have access to U.S. courts, the Defense Department established the Combatant Status Review Tribunal. The Defense Department informed suspected terrorists that they may use U.S. courts to contest their detentions and that they could challenge their status as enemy combatants before a military tribunal called the Combatant Status Review Tribunal.

released, transferred to his home country, or returned to his cell. Once again, final judgment rests with the defense secretary.

Supreme Court Rulings

Debates over Guantánamo Bay detention policies have raged on continuously since before the first flight of captives took off from the airstrip in Kandahar, Afghanistan. The three key legal issues are prisoner of war status versus enemy-combatant status, the rights of detainees held at Gitmo to plead their cases in U.S. courts, and the U.S. president's power to make these decisions without holding trials. Supporters of each side have made their arguments in the media, before Congress, and in the lower-level courtrooms. In April 2004, the U.S. Supreme Court heard two cases regarding the detention of enemy combatants, and the court's decisions on June 28, 2004, may force sweeping changes to the Bush administration's current policies on this matter.

BACK TO THE BATTLEFIELD

The detainee review process, although complex and lengthy, is necessary to ensure that only those men who truly pose a threat to the United States and its allies remain at Gitmo. But as thorough as the interrogation and review process is, serious risk remains. U.S. military intelligence officials now believe several detainees released from Gitmo have returned to the fight against coalition forces. In one case, senior Taliban commander Mullah Shehzada convinced interrogators he was an innocent Afghan citizen and was released from Gitmo in July 2003. Shehzada reportedly took over Taliban operations against U.S. forces in southern Afghanistan and, in October 2003, led a jailbreak during which forty-one Taliban prisoners burrowed their way to freedom.

Each case combined two similar lawsuits that the Supreme Court addressed singularly in the interest of limited time. The first case is *Rasul v. Bush* (docket #03-334) and *Al Odah v. United States* (docket #03-343), which the Supreme Court heard on April 20, 2004. Representing British, Australian, and Kuwaiti citizens, the case argued that foreign nationals held at Gitmo should have access to challenge their detention in U.S. civilian courts. The Supreme Court ruled 6-3 in favor of the detainees. This decision negates the Bush administration's argument that Cuba's sovereignty over Guantánamo Bay overrides U.S. court jurisdiction. This could open the door to potentially hundreds of cases dealing with civil-liberties objections to detention and treatment.

U.S. Secretary of Defense Donald H. Rumsfeld (*center*) visits Gitmo on January 2, 2002. Brigadier General Michael R. Lehnert, Joint Task Force 160 commander (*left*) and Major General Gary D. Speer, assistant commander in chief, U.S. Southern Command (*right*) gave Secretary Rumsfeld a tour of the Gitmo facility. During the visit Secretary Rumsfeld explained that Taliban and Al Qaeda detainees would not be given prisoner of war status.

The second case, *Padilla v. Rumsfeld* (docket #03-1027) and *Hamdi v. Rumsfeld* (docket #03-6696), involves two U.S. citizens, both suspected Al Qaeda supporters, and was presented on April 28, 2004. José Padilla, an Islam convert known as Abdullah Al Muhajir, was apprehended in Chicago, Illinois, on suspicion of plotting a dirty bomb attack on U.S. soil. A dirty bomb is a conventional bomb, made with explosives such as dynamite, which is wrapped with radioactive material to cause greater death and injury. Yaser Hamdi, who was born in Louisiana while his Saudi Arabian

father was working in the United States, was captured in an Afghanistan battle zone armed with an assault rifle. Padilla is in detention on a military base in Charleston, South Carolina, under conditions similar to those at Gitmo.

The U.S. Supreme Court ruled 8-1 that the U.S. Congress granted President Bush authority to label U.S. citizens enemy combatants when it passed Joint Resolution 23 on September 18, 2001. However, in the same decision, the Supreme Court ruled that Hamdi had the right to challenge his detention in U.S. courts. Padilla's case was thrown out because the Supreme Court determined that his lawsuit was not filed in the correct jurisdiction—his lawyers filed his case in New York, but they should have filed in the state in which he is being detained. Padilla filed a new case in a lower South Carolina court in July 2004. In September 2004, after the Supreme Court's June decision, the U.S. government decided to release Hamdi, allowing him to return to Saudi Arabia in October without facing charges.

An immediate outcome of the Supreme Court decisions was the formation of the Combatant Status Review Tribunal (CSRT). To ensure that only those detainees deemed enemy combatants are held at Gitmo, on July 7, 2004, the U.S. Department of Defense established a new initial screening process called the Combatant Status Review Tribunal. This review process is very similar to that of the existing annual detainee review. Secretary of the Navy Gordon R. England was appointed by Deputy Secretary of Defense Paul Wolfowitz to lead the tribunals. Each tribunal is made up of three neutral officers who have not been involved in the detainee's capture and imprisonment. After an official review of all the information related to the designation of a detainee as an enemy combatant, the tribunal reports its decision on the detainee's status in writing to Navy Rear Admiral James M. McGarrah. Detainees deemed enemy combatants are held at Gitmo for interrogation and pending military commissions; those deemed noncombatants would be released to their home countries. By October 1, 2004, Admiral McGarrah had reviewed sixty-four of the 115 completed CSRTs. Of sixty-four detainees, only one was determined not to be an enemy combatant. The DOD expects to conduct CSRTs for all current Gitmo detainees by the end of 2004.

Indefinite Detention

The Geneva Conventions exist to ensure that detainees held outside the combat zone are free from torture and humiliation and that they are repatriated (returned home) when the warring forces agree to end the conflict. However, when international law is disrespected or ignored, the rules of war no longer apply. This is the situation faced by the United States in its war on terrorism and, consequently, by the enemy combatants detained at Guantánamo Bay.

Military commissions and annual reviews bring a degree of order to the Gitmo detention situation, but they may not silence the controversy over detainee rights. Military commissions are structured to try detainees for war crimes, not for the threat of perpetuating future terrorist acts on the United States and its allies. It is conceivable that a detainee can be acquitted, or cleared, of war crimes by the commission but still pose a threat in the eyes of the annual review board. He would likely remain in detention. In a November 2004 federal court decision, which could set precedent for future review tribunals and commissions, U.S. District Judge James Robertson ruled the review process incompetent in the case of Salim Ahmed Hamdan. Robertson said Hamdan should not be subject to a military commission unless a competent tribunal determines he is not entitled to prisoner of war status. The U.S. Justice Department plans to appeal Robertson's ruling on the grounds that the Geneva Conventions do not apply to Al Qaeda members.

Back in September 2003, a reporter at CBS News asked Sergeant Major John Van Natta, a warden at Camp Delta, if this could be a life sentence for some detainees. Van Natta replied, "It very likely could be."

Glossary

Al Qaeda An Arabic word meaning "the foundation," Al Qaeda is an independent military organization that is heavily influenced by its interpretation of the Islamic religion. Established by Osama bin Laden in 1988, it is widely regarded as a terrorist organization. Other common English spellings include "al Qaida" and "al Queda."

coalition A group of nations that have offered various degrees of political and military support to the United States for the 2001 invasion of Afghanistan and the 2003 invasion of Iraq. Great Britain has been the most supportive American ally.

commute To substitute one punishment in the place of another.

court proceeding The sequence of steps taken in matters of law, such as a criminal trial. Legal judgments, jury verdicts, and commission decisions are the result of these steps.

defer To postpone or delay to a later time.

Ex Parte Quirin The 1942 U.S. Supreme Court ruling held as precedent for the use of military commissions at Gitmo. The Supreme Court affirmed that the U.S. president could try eight German saboteurs, captured trying to enter the United States with bomb-detonating materials, in a military tribunal without a jury. The defendants were German citizens, yet all had spent time living in the United States.

fundamentalist movement Islamic fundamentalism is the belief by Muslims that the true interpretation of the Koran must rely solely on the Koran and the prophetic Hadith, or oral accounts of Muhammad's teachings and practices. Wahhabism is a fundamentalist movement of the Sunni form of Islam and is claimed to be the religious movement that Osama bin Laden follows.

Geneva Conventions Treaties formulated between 1864 and 1949 in Geneva, Switzerland, that set the standards for international law for human concerns. Accusations of violation on the part of party nations are brought before the International Court of Justice at the Hague in the Netherlands.

interrogation The professional police and military technique of interviewing people, permitted by the laws of war, often without the people's consent, to obtain information regarding crimes or military operations.

Islam An Arabic word meaning "submission (to God)" and described as a way of life and/or religion. Followers of Islam are known as Muslims, who practice the religious teachings of Muhammad that are contained in the Koran.

jurisdiction The area to which the executive or legislative powers or laws of a government extend, that is, their geographical or national boundaries of authority.

military courts-martial Military courts that determine punishments for members of the military subject to military law. (The singular form is court-martial.)

military tribunal (or military commission) A judicial proceeding that operates outside the scope of criminal and civil matters, with military officials serving as judges and jurors. Tribunals are often executed with a degree of secrecy.

mitigate To make less severe or painful.

Operation Sea Signal From August 1994 to February 1996, navy personnel based at Gitmo and marines from II Marine Expeditionary Force assumed the mission of feeding, housing, clothing, and caring for more than 50,000 Haitian and Cuban migrants seeking asylum in the United States.

operative A person secretly employed in espionage for a government or other organization.

Pentagon The headquarters of the U.S. Department of Defense, which is located just outside Washington, D.C.

sovereignty Government of a country or territory that is free from external control.

Taliban Pashtun, meaning "religious student," the Taliban is an oppressive Islamist movement that ruled most of Afghanistan from 1996 to 2001, despite diplomatic recognition from only three countries, and that forged an alliance with Al Qaeda.

terrorism Commonly used term to refer to the calculated use of violence or the threat of violence against a civilian population for the purpose of producing fear, usually for some political end. An active participant in an act of terrorism is a terrorist.

U.S. criminal court system Criminal courts deal with actions considered harmful to society. In criminal cases, the government takes legal action against an individual. Sentences range from probation and fines to imprisonment and, in some cases, death.

U.S. Southern Command Headquartered in Miami, Florida, the U.S. Southern Command is responsible for all U.S. military activities on the landmass of Latin America south of Mexico, the waters adjacent to Central and South America, the

Caribbean Sea, and parts of the Atlantic Ocean.

U.S. Supreme Court The highest federal court in the United States, it has ultimate judicial authority within the country to interpret and decide questions of all American laws. It is the only court required by the U.S. Constitution and has jurisdiction over all other courts in the nation.

war on terrorism Referring to several government initiatives and military actions primarily advanced by the United States to reduce the threat of global terrorism in the wake of Al Qaeda attacks on U.S. targets on September 11, 2001.

For More Information

American Red Cross
  National Headquarters
2025 E Street NW
Washington, DC 20006
Phone: (202) 303-4498
Web site: http://www.redcross.org

Amnesty International USA
322 Eighth Avenue
New York, NY 10001
Phone: (212) 807-8400
Web site: http://www.
  amnestyusa.org

Human Rights Watch
350 Fifth Avenue
34th Floor
New York, NY 10118-3299
(212) 290-4700
Web site: http://www.hrwnyc@
  hrw.org

Naval Base Guantánamo Bay
PSC 1005 Box 25
FPO, AE 09593
Web site: http://www.nsgtmo.
  navy.mil

United States Southern Command
3511 NW Ninety-first Avenue
Miami, FL 33172-1217
Toll Free: (888) 547-4025
Web site: http://www.southcom.mil

U.S. Department of Homeland
    Security
Washington, DC 20528
Web site: http://www.dhs.gov/
    dhspublic/index.jsp

U.S. Department of Justice
950 Pennsylvania Avenue NW

Washington, DC 20530-0001
Web site: http://www.usdoj.gov

Web Sites

Due to the changing nature of
Internet links, the Rosen
Publishing Group, Inc., has
developed an online list of Web
sites related to the subject of this
book. This site is updated regu-
larly. Please use this link to
access the list:

http://www.rosenlinks.com/fcce/gbmt

For Further Reading

Berkowitz, Bruce D. *The New
    Face of War: How War Will be
    Fought in the 21st Century.*
    New York: Free Press, 2003.
Burnett, Betty. *The Attack on
    the USS Cole in Yemen on
    October 12, 2000.* (Terrorist
    Attacks). New York: The
    Rosen Publishing Group,
    Inc., 2003.

Fiscus, James W. *America's War in
    Afghanistan.* (War and Conflict
    in the Middle East). New York:
    The Rosen Publishing Group,
    Inc., 2004.
Gard, Carolyn. *The Attack on the
    Pentagon on September 11,
    2001.* (Terrorist Attacks). New
    York: The Rosen Publishing
    Group, Inc., 2003.

Gard, Carolyn. *The Attacks on the World Trade Center: February 26, 1993 and September 11, 2001*. (Terrorist Attacks). New York: The Rosen Publishing Group, Inc., 2003.

Margulies, Phillip. *Al Qaeda: Osama bin Laden's Army of Terrorists*. (Inside the World's Most Infamous Terrorist Organization). New York: The Rosen Publishing Group, Inc., 2003.

Olshansky, Barbara. *Secret Trials and Executions: Military Tribunals and the Threat to Democracy*. New York: Seven Stories Press, 2002.

U.S. Department of Defense. Military Commission Instructions. Retrieved May 2004 (http://www. defenselink.milnews/ commissions.html).

Bibliography

Associated Press. "Brief History of Guantánamo Bay." December 28, 2001. Retrieved February 2004 (http://www.foxnews.com/ story/0,2933,41744,00.html).

Associated Press. "U.S.' Detention of Teens Condemned." November 30, 2003. Retrieved February 2004 (http://www. taipeitimes.com/News/world/ archives/2003/11/30/ 2003077836).

CNN.com. "Shackled Detainees Arrive in Guantánamo." Retrieved November 2004 (http://archives.cnn.com/2002/ world/asiapcf/central/01/11/ret. detainee.transfer),

Department of Defense News Release. *The Pentagon Has Announced the First Charges*

Against Foreign Detainees at Guantánamo Bay in Cuba. February 24, 2004.

Department of Defense Press Conference Transcript. *Announcements of Key Personnel for Military Commissions; Issuance of Military Commission Instruction No. 9 on Military Commissions Review Panel.* December 30, 2003.

Department of Defense Press Conference Transcript. *Briefing on Detainee Operations at Guantánamo Bay.* February 13, 2004.

Gearan, Anne. "Supreme Court Mulls Enemy Combatant Case." Associated Press, February 4, 2004. Retrieved February 2004 (http://www.worldwire.org/worldnews/article8556.htm).

Greene, Richard Allen. *Analysis: Military Tribunals.* BBC News, March 4, 2003. Retrieved February 2004 (http://news.bbc.co.uk/1/hi/world/americas1701789.stm).

Hirsh, Michael. *At War with Ourselves: Why America Is Squandering Its Chance to Build a Better World.* New York: Oxford University Press, 2003.

Kozaryn, Linda D. "Detainees Important to Intelligence Effort, Rumsfeld Says." American Forces Press Service, February 16, 2004.

Lewis, Neal A., and Eric Schmitt. "Cuba Detentions May Last Years." *New York Times,* February 12, 2004.

Merriman, Rima. "Intelligence Gathering and Due Process Are at Odds in the U.S." *Jordan Times,* February 9, 2004.

Sontag, Deborah. "Terror Suspect's Path from Streets to Brig." *New York Times,* April 25, 2004.

Starr, Barbara. "Review Panel to Oversee Guantanamo Tribunals." CNN.com, December 29, 2003. Retrieved November 2004 (http://www.cnn.com/2003/LAW/12/29/military.commissions).

Index

A

Abu Ghraib prison, 16
Al Qaeda, 11, 15, 17, 18–19, 20, 21, 27, 28, 37, 39
annual detainee reviews, 33, 34–35, 36, 38

B

Bahlul, Ali Hamza Ahmed Sulayman al-, 29
bin Laden, Osama, 11, 15, 17, 19
Bush, President George W., 4, 15, 19, 26, 27, 37

C

Castro, Fidel, 10
Combatant Status Review Tribunal, 38
Criminal Investigative Task Force, 28

E

England, Gordon R., 38
Ex Parte Quirin, 15, 29–30

G

Geneva Conventions, 4, 13, 14–15, 16, 17, 19, 39

Guantánamo Bay
accommodations for detainees at, 23–25
debates over detention policies, 35
detainee-screening process and transfer to, 21–22
establishment of detention center at, 9–12
establishment of U.S. naval base at, 8
history of, 6, 7–9

H

Hamdi, Yaser, 37, 38
Hamdi v. Rumsfeld, 37
Hood, Jay W., 16

J

Joint Resolution, 23, 37
Joint Task Forces 160 and 170, 10, 28

M

McGarrah, James M., 38
Military Commission Instructions, 31–32
military tribunals
explanation of, 26
procedures of, 27–29, 30–31
who faces, 27–29

Miller, Geoffrey, 16

O

Odah, Al, v. United States, 36
Operation Sea Signal, 10

P

Padilla, José, 37
Padilla v. Rumsfeld, 37–38
prisoners of war, classification of, 14–15, 17, 19

Q

Qosi, Ibrahim Ahmed Mahmoud al-, 11, 29

R

Rasul v. Bush, 36
Rumsfeld, Donald H., 9, 29, 33

S

Shehzada, Mullah, 36
Spanish-American War, 8

T

Taliban, 15, 17–18, 19, 20, 21, 36
Treaty of 1934, 8

W

Wahhabism, 17
Wolfowitz, Paul, 38

About the Author

Bill Scheppler is an award-winning freelance writer who has written on subjects ranging from the Internet to the Ironman, from Special Forces to civil rights. *Guantánamo Bay and Military Tribunals* is Scheppler's fifth book written for the Rosen Publishing Group. Scheppler holds a bachelor's degree in history, and currently lives in the San Francisco Bay area with his wife, Emily.

Photo Credits

Cover, pp. 22, 26 © AP/Wide World Photos; pp. 4–5, 27, 30 © Joe Raedle/Getty Images; p. 6 © EPA/US Navy/AP/Wide World Photos; pp. 7, 14 © Bettmann/Corbis; p. 8 Library of Congress Geography and Map Division; p. 9 © Bill Gentile/Corbis; p. 12 Staff Sgt. Stephen Lewald/US Army/DoD; pp. 12 (inset), 13, 28 © Reuters/Corbis; p. 16 © Sean Ramsay/Getty Images; p. 18 © Corbis Sygma; p. 20 © Scott Nelson, Pool/AP/Wide World Photos; pp. 24, 37 © Joshua S. Higgins/USMC/Getty Images; p. 25 Seaman David P. Coleman/US Navy/DoD; p. 33 © Petty Officer 1st Class Shane T. McCoy/US Navy/Getty Images; p. 35 © Randall Damm/AFP/Getty Images.

Design: Geri Fletcher; **Editor:** Kathy Kuhtz Campbell; **Photo Researcher:** Amy Feinberg